Poetry

Wideawake Field

*I Am the Beggar of the World: Landays from
Contemporary Afghanistan* (translator)

Nonfiction

*The Tenth Parallel: Dispatches from the
Fault Line Between Christianity and Islam*

*Amity and Prosperity: One Family
and the Fracturing of America*

IF MEN,
THEN

ELIZA GRISWOLD

IF MEN, THEN

FARRAR STRAUS GIROUX

NEW YORK

Farrar, Straus and Giroux
120 Broadway, New York 10271

Grateful acknowledgment is made to the publications in
which versions of the following poems originally appeared:
Granta: "Friday Afternoon with Boko Haram"; *The Independent*:
"Host"; *The New Yorker*: "Reflect," "A Rock Rolled Out of Bed,"
"Hurt People," "Of Empty Heaven and Its Hymns," "Old School,"
"The Morning After," "Singer Futura," "Cookie," and "Towed";
The Paris Review: "Goodbye, Mullah Omar"; *Poetry*: "Pulling
Out," "Water Table," "Ruins," "Geographic," "Lampedusa,"
"Netherworld Weathergirl," "Testing," and "Libyan Proverbs."

Library of Congress Control Number: 2019952156
ISBN: 978-0-374-28077-2

Designed by Crisis

Our books may be purchased in bulk for promotional,
educational, or business use. Please contact your local bookseller
or the Macmillan Corporate and Premium Sales Department
at 1-800-221-7945, extension 5442, or by e-mail at
MacmillanSpecialMarkets@macmillan.com.

www.fsgbooks.com
www.twitter.com/fsgbooks
www.facebook.com/fsgbooks

1 3 5 7 9 10 8 6 4 2

Of what was it I was thinking?
So the meaning escapes.

WALLACE STEVENS,
"Metaphors of a Magnifico"

CONTENTS

3

4

IF MEN,
THEN

PRAYER

What can we offer the child
at the border: a river of shoes,
her coat stitched with coins,
her father killed for his teeth,
her mother, sewing her
daughter's future into a hem.

Alone, but for a brother who shoves her
ahead through the barbed-wire fence,
knowing she's safer without him—
a truth she cannot yet fathom,
being too young for the ways of men.

Nothing is what we can offer.
The child died years ago.
Except practice a finer caliber of kindness
to the stranger rather than wield
this burden of self, this harriedness.
Humility involves less us.

PRELUDE TO A MASSACRE

Twenty men crossing a bridge,
into a village,
is not a metaphor
but prelude to a massacre.

Marred by violence,
my mind begs forgiveness,
self-conscious at its pattern of reprise.

This old song can't stop singing itself:

If men,
Then . . .

The bright clatter of boots
on the slats of a bridge,
the mustachioed laughs,
the rise of the first lime-
washed wall of the village,
and behind the wall, women
pinning laundry to a wire.

GOODBYE, MULLAH OMAR

Wormwood grows on the one-eyed Mullah's grave.
The Talib boys fight blindly on believing he's alive.
—Anonymous

Charlie says when Afghan men get together,
the number of eyes is always odd.

A generation has outdated wounds.
No longer cool, or relevant, the Taliban

can't muster the fear they used to.
The duffers stalk the graveyard and the chowk,

finger their hennaed beards. They cultivate cartoon.
Once, a deaf-mute pressed her thumb to chin

to warn me they were coming,
the universal symbol, Fear the Beard.

There's ancient precedent for their love
of the fore-flattened image.

In medieval painting, failure is a prayer.
To render perspective less precisely

indicates humility.
The bowed head knows its flaws.

The land belongs to ISIS now.
No one settles for an eye;

how quaint, how Deuteronomy.
The depiction that matters

is inflicting suffering on others.
Where are your scars

Where are your scars now,
Where are your scars now, wonderboys?

KALIYUGA

According to seven-thousand-year-old holy texts of the Vedas, we're now living in Kaliyuga—the last of the four yugas, or ages—and known as the age of degeneration for its greed, conflict, inequality, droughts, and floods. Scholars contest its beginning, but many mark the start about five thousand years ago, and predict that it will continue for 427,000 years.

It's not the goddess Kali but
a throw of the dice, a toss,
and luck.
       Not fate, or any other
greater order, flings up the world
to come down on its edge,
at odds, existence teetering.

We lovers of the liminal delight
in conflagration, set up
our beach chairs at the battle side.

HOST

In eastern Congo years ago on a road logged into a hill
we drove or were driven one evening to meet pygmies
who claimed they were being eaten, which was possible.
A woman with my name had watched the fire
on which her arm was cooked and then devoured.
The pygmies turned out to be lying and this isn't about
    pygmies.
In the truck we argued with the driver about gays and the
    Bible
as we lurched through the intestinal dark
toward the safe haven of a Catholic priest
who fed us the baby chimpanzee we'd seen
when we'd pulled up that afternoon
fighting his tether on the Father's porch.

FRIDAY AFTERNOON WITH BOKO HARAM

We spent the Hezbollah war in Nigeria
eating hummus in a Syrian café and watching rockets.
Nights alone in a hotel in Kano, we saw a girl grow
famous on TV. We almost died in the North, you know.
But you don't, no one does, except the photographer
who crouched shotgun and begged the mob
with hammered swords for his camera and passport.
Its folio of spent pages, like the ordered laws of nations,
was as irrelevant as our heads would be
once cleaved from our pleading bodies.
We'd be flung between them until one boy
got bored and tossed us into the sopping dirt.
The young blonde hosts a special now on what to do in
    Dubai;
that obscene indoor ski slope, jeeps that bounce
like jelly donuts over dunes lit to look friendly.
There must be so many of us, spies who are really
    academics,
checking into obscure hotels, ordering contraband beer.
Hating ourselves, we pick at what swells till the larvae
embedded in our backs hatch out of the skin,
till moths escape, subcutaneous angels.

GAIA

In 1979, James Lovelock published the Gaia hypothesis,
which posits the world is a single living organism
and possesses the ability to regulate itself.

Fragments of men who meant to be better,
are you doing the work of our world,
riddled with woes, as she ushers
us off her surface? Has she come to you
offering a glimpse of heaven
in return for dispatching the rest of us
faster than cancer?

The Gaia hypothesis holds that the earth
is a body possessing the means to rid itself
of aggressors and malignancies.

Viewed in this manner, we are
the slow-growing cancer, and the boys'
quicker work is to eradicate us.

PULLING OUT

Exodus is a traffic jam,
and traffic jams are dangerous.

Ahead of us, armed with sticks and rakes,
a child's brigade does battle

on this doomed track hourly blown to dust.
To occupy themselves, they race a tank.

Dust is faster. Tattered surveillance blimps
yank against steel tethers over the salt-lick plain.

The road goes boom again. The flimsy means
by which we try to distance war

don't matter anymore. Disguise your car,
your hair, take to the air, stare down

on the terrible mirror of the ground
where those who didn't qualify

for tickets to the sky
wave goodbye, goodbye.

WATER TABLE

My earliest wish was not to exist—
to burst in the backyard
behind the rectory
where no one would see me.
This wasn't a plea to be found
or mourned for, but to be unborn
into the atmosphere. To hang
in the humid air, as ponds vent upward
from the overheated earth,
rise until they freeze
and crystallize, then drop
into the aquifer.

ON WEARING A TRACKING DEVICE

The rechargeable heart, a pulse
of blue light, flickers against
my breastbone's hollow—
a signal for a rental satellite
that follows for a day or two
until the signal dies.

We have reasons for moving.

We've hurtled toward disaster
to practice moving faster
than regular living allows.

Proof of movement isn't proof of life.

HABEAS CORPUS

Eaglewood, agarwood, jinko, oud
are names for the same precious infection
that grows in Asian evergreens.
Indifferent to its host, the resin's rare,
a costly gift for a mother
to press into the palm of strangers
she hopes may free her son
from Guantánamo.

       The little that we strangers
       knew of motherhood was rooted
       in the misguided belief that
       one body could grow another
       when and how it wanted.
       No one knew for sure where
       her boy was. Who knows now.

RUINS

A spring day oozes through Trastevere.
A nun in turquoise sneakers
contemplates the stairs.

Every hard bulb stirs.

The egg in our chest cracks
against our will.

The dead man on the Congo road
was missing an ear,
which had been eaten
or someone was wearing
it around his neck.

The dead man looked like this, no, that.
Here's a flock of tourists
in matching canvas hats.
We're healing by mistake.
Rome is also built on ruins.

GEOGRAPHIC

            Lampedusa,
let us find in your deprivation our love
of deprivation, in your bleakness
our bleakness, in your frank cliffs
the same. Teach us to align
            our will with what is.

LAMPEDUSA

*Over the past decade, hundreds of thousands of African migrants
have traveled from Libya to the island of Lampedusa, off the
coast of Italy, on their journey northward to Europe.*

The groaning boats pull in, gunwales
sunk by the weight of flight. Above
the water line, each pitching prow
reveals an evil eye. Friends who call
across the harbor, *Where are we,*
before you rejoice here's our advice:
be grateful for your fake-fur parka,
the wheelie bag you drag with the snow-
suited baby. In the defunct bunkers
on this tropical rock, the island's out
of water. The shore bears a cross
nailed from the ribs of sunken ships,
rubber shoes, scraps of scrawled prayer—
one million calls to the wrong God.
And you, giddy with surviving war
elsewhere, unsure whom to please,
grin at every face and wave desperately
down at the skiff we rented to reach you before

the police. Take care. We offer less help than
we seem to. Don't trust us. Spell out
a fake name. Go north. Stay off the train.

EARLY MIDDLE AGES

Once upon a time, rats
on grain ships out of Egypt
bound for the starved Empire
carried bubo-stricken fleas.
Nowadays we export them
in 4-wheel wheel wells
shipped from Tennessee
to Turkey to be resold
on battlefields. Did you hear
about the plumber in Texas
forced to shut his shop after his truck
showed up on TV, property of ISIS? Rats
in the wheel wells, always rats
and sickness, and the weakness
that building walls implies, and skies,
now empty of starlings, wheel themselves.

2

FIRST PERSON

The first person's always last to know.

I

REFLECT

I is a lion
who snarls
at the lion
in the water
who snarls.

II

THERE IS NO WE IN KALIYUGA

I is better at endings. You're beginning,
you and she, here in the ever after—

you, whoever you may be,
and I, the unknown entity
returning from a front.

The war we started elsewhere
is here in this era of degeneration,
of CBD and NDAs;

of armored SUVs as four-door fantasies
in which to outrun apocalypse, replete
with solar chargers, iodine,
inflatables endorsed by SEALs—

accoutrements for go bags packed
by those of us high
from having made it through the day.

III

NETHERWORLD WEATHERGIRL

The pack is filing from I's nowheresvilles,
filling the halfway hotels, calling each other
by satellite, a dollar per minute to say hello.
At home, I tries to grow a new life
among others bored by the womb.
Who has time to run a thumb between her legs
and calculate temperature—
netherworld weathergirl, chipper, bitter.

IV

TESTING

I

Body,
      you and I are inhospitable
in another era pitiable

in this one perhaps
      powerful.

Have you earned the right
      to blow yourself up

are you I's fault are you
      her salvation

or nothing
         to worry about?

II

When he said no,
                    I went for his dresser,
          opened the top drawer,
broke the paper seals
          on the two sterile cups,
and wiped her dirty
                    thumbs inside.

Because their stubborn love
          won't die, I had to kill it,
will it dead. Or so
          she thought until I passed
                    a cycle on her own.
          He doesn't know
                    what's grown
                              inside I
          since she bled.

V

GREEN

I shouldered her hobo sorrow and soldiered on.
She was warden of an angry garden,
guarding against what hoped to grow.
The bitter bud that never opens hardens.

VI

Before I died, she came to me
saying she'd stumbled on
the universe's secret, stubbed
her toe so many times on a rock
in the road, the rock rolled out
of its bed, crying, *Woman,*
is it never enough?!

I peered at the rock, studied its face,
maybe its belly. Did it have a tiny
mouth where all the rigid principles
that rule the galaxy dissolve?

No way to tell. The quarks
had pulled themselves together.
In Revelation, when the white stone deigns
to speak, it offers a new name.

One came. Had it spoken?
Or was her bothered brain
more broken than she'd feared?
I straightened up.

VII

HURT PEOPLE

Troubled, I goes to the doctor
who asks her to draw herself
with a Crayola marker. I sketches
Cotton Mather. Puritans are chic,
three centuries on, their strictures
ripe for redemption.

Turns out the things they did
and said aren't all that bad
in the light of what they'd fled.
Hurt people hurt people.

Cotton and his father Increase
conjured the Salem tribunals.
Later Cotton tried to claim
he'd never attended an execution,
but he'd been spotted jeering
in the mob, exhorting
a drowning woman to fly.

VIII

OF EMPTY HEAVEN AND ITS HYMNS

I doesn't dream.
She doesn't seem
to have a sleeping state.

High-strung, hyper-vigilant,
she's one plucked nerve
away from springing
free of struts and frets.

Which might be wonderful.

The man who plays the blue guitar
doesn't care what happens to his strings.
Disposable as instrument,
I sings herself hoarse.

Late at night, she jokes
among the other frayed strings,
Cat gut my tongue.

IX

BEMBIX

One of 380 species of predatory sand wasps, Bembix boharti
Griswold *was identified in 1983 in the Sea of Cortez.*

I searched for herself on the Sea of Cortez
among the scald of light and salt
and later, in a book, she found

a sand wasp named for her:
Bembix boharti Griswold,
which burrows into a blasted arroyo,
and buries eggs with strong hind legs,
setting in motion a clutch
of improbable lives.

I's zodiac proved indestructible,
the rubber raft was reinforced
to scrape along a rocky bottom,
which was good, because I was.

X

OLD SCHOOL

I is pre-millennial, and so
much of what forged her
is actionable now: the Fox News guy
slipping his phone number
over the anchor's desk,
below the camera's eye;
the radio host calling her a failure
for becoming a mother. The time
she was shamed for wearing a burka.

At lunch last week a board member
guessed at her weight, pitting her
against his eighty-pound doodle.
What's to be said? Since none
of these moments mattered,
or seemed to when the body
was a distraction, an impediment
to getting things done, which I did.

XI

THE MORNING AFTER

After I left the land of wine-soaked solace,
she sought another kind of chaos.

Insisting on sadness, on seeking the world
as it is, she called Dionysus,

the morning after,
bits of mysterious skin

in his tannin-stained teeth—
vegetable, animal, grape, human;

there was no way of being certain
what he'd bitten into.

Who's calling?, he roared,
half-serious, knowing rage

is comic at its height, and I,
ardent scribe, bristled with thrill

and tugged out her notebook,
eager to share any awful story.

XII

Before the word disposable
became immoral, nothing
was forever—
not Styrofoam or time:
Not money, and not I.
I didn't intend to last.
She depended on not lasting.
Disappearing's tougher
than it seems.

        Then there were three.
        I alone was gone,
        cover blown, no more
        moping in the coffee shop.
        She stopped not trying
        to die exactly, but she gave up
        the dream of giving up.

XIII

I is instinct gone awry. Sugar,
speed, near death, she loved
to limn oblivion, thrived
off the grid, since the grid
was fraught with dead ideas
of what a life should be.

In her inherited America,
mothers don't risk
their skins. They monogram and fold.

XIV

COOKIE

I jokes she's a Scout
knocking on your soul's door
with one free offer
or another, maybe a tote.

And you, supposed master
of evasive maneuver, peer
through the blinds, feigning absence.

Still, all smiles, she persists.

You might try the Cheshire manner
of refusal, half grin, half grimace
same aim of disappearance.

Unfazed, I will press her face
to the pane and wait.

Holding tight to the wall,
you'll have to drop and crawl
to the toilet at some point.

I knows. She's already earned
her badge in you.

XV

TOWED

I understands how you might feel
that where she parked the car
reveals a kind of disregard
bordering on disrespect.

You didn't say or have to say
as much—it was the way
your eyelids fluttered near each
other in caress, as if to arm

your consciousness against
expressing exasperation
at the continual arrival
of unpredictable events

that come along with I.
Much like the world
destabilized by rising
temperatures and seas,

I can approach
catastrophe, a carnival
whack-a-mole
run amok. I is sorry.

3

ODE TO THE PEOPLE OF MELOS

In 431 BC, the Athenians also made an expedition against the isle
of Melos with thirty ships of their own, six Chian, and two
Lesbian vessels, sixteen hundred heavy infantry, three hundred
archers, and twenty mounted archers from Athens, and about
fifteen hundred heavy infantry from the allies and the islanders.
—Thucydides, *History of the Peloponnesian War*

Be reasonable, the Athenians
told the people of Melos. Can't you see
the forest of masts in your harbor,
the glint of our armor flashing over
the waves? There's no dishonor in surrender
when defeat unfurls its tattered flag.
Your gods are nothing now.

No, the people of Melos replied,
like most who would follow. We insist
on bloodshed as a matter of honor,
and our children's after.

Thus Melos was besieged, and though
its people managed twice to break

the blockade and seize some corn,
later the Athenians put grown men
to death, sold off the women,
    and lived in the houses left for them.

GONE THE LOFTY DAYS OF PERICLES

Our heroes dig ditches.
We cheer them as they knock
the bodies in. This wasn't

the Athens Pericles foresaw. *We
in Athens live exactly as we please
while Sparta proves its painful*

manliness. No more lauding citizens
for their taste in furnishings.

The mob at the crowd's edge
waits for the end of the speech
to rush in and dismember the speaker.

We are Spartans now.

LIBYAN PROVERBS

from One Hundred Arabic Proverbs from Libya,
*translated by Mohamed Abdelkafi and purchased in a hotel gift shop
in Tripoli in 2006, five years before Muammar Qaddafi fell*

The naked man in the caravan

     has peace of mind. He whose covering

          belongs to others is uncovered.

       He who has luck will have the winds

         blow him his firewood.

     He whose trousers are made of dry grass should
     not warm himself

        at the fire.
He howled before going mad.

       He led the lion by the ear.

Like the sparrow, he wanted to imitate

the pigeon's walk but lost his own.

Walk with sandals till you get good shoes.

Where the turban moves, there moves

the territory. Men meet

but mountains don't. Always taking out

without giving back, even the mountains

will be broken. Penny piled on penny

makes a heap. Only the unlucky coin

is left in the purse. As long as a human
being lives

he learns.

Learn to shave by shaving orphans.

He who is to be hanged may insult the Pasha.

In the house of a man who has been hanged

don't speak of rope.

My belly before my children.

ODE TO THE DEAD JOURNALIST

in memoriam Kim Wall, 1987–2017

1

She might've feared the billionaire
who'd built a leaky submarine;
otherwise, it seemed a low-risk trip
under the Køge Bay, descending
for a day into the murk—
an unspoken transaction
as all such discussions are,
the cost of paying attention
of being paid attention to.

2

We compete. We do.
We race to places faster and after,
judge the other's page—
huh, that's all she got—
yet offer our last Tampax,

dearer than the ten thousand crisp dollars
with serial numbers after 2015
we also hand over.

3

When we die, all
pettiness dissolves.
We form a furious army
that stares down the Elah Valley
at a figure eight feet tall
clad in brass and swinging
his sword and balls around.
One stone brings him down.

BAKER'S TOMB, 30 BC

The baker Eurysaces built a monument
to suffering. A former slave,
he bought his flesh with sweat.
His grave, a marble oven,
shelters pigeons
in a Roman roundabout.

Knapsacks burdened with ambition,
we were terrible fellows,
unwilling to accept
the less hope of success
the more room for the soul.

Who cared for the soul?
The soul would come later,
or never—its knowledge born
of failure. We weren't born to fail.

Our will was all we knew
and we raged at a world
that wouldn't give against it.
Eurysaces the audacious dared
to immortalize the unglamorous
daily devotion that saved him.

WAITING FOR THE VOLCANO

Our high-speed hydrofoil is late.
We wait in the island's worst places,
Aeolian churches. Bartholomew,
an aging patron saint, drapes
flayed skin across one arm,
a sommelier or a thespian.
Harrowing renders us raw;
it also frees a captive field to sprout.
There's nowhere on this island
that doesn't turn us more against
ourselves or one another—too many
days in paradise for minds like ours.

REMEDY

after Ovid's Remedia Amoris

Don't begin. Raging rivers grow
from springs. Don't eat arugula
or other spicy things. Cling to every awfulness:
rank breath, bad sex, even if it never was. (Ovid is
this crude.) Beware of solitude. Love your rival.
Take another lover. Splitting a river
cuts its flow. Go fishing. Go to the farm.
Fling your seed in any upturned soil.
Avoid the plague of idleness.
Don't play dice, sleep greedily,
fuddle your temples with wine.
Drink none or to oblivion.

APOTHEOSIS

To return to that time is to enter a tomb
in which bewildered dead wander
clutching paper Gucci loafers, gifts
of over-leveraged descendants who come
bearing luxury grave goods, and in want.
The dead can't hear pleas, no matter how dear.
Having neither ears nor feet, ghosts lurch
in unmeasured beats, as the drunk do.
In Rome you and I tried to fashion a foundation
from the rubble of unfinished lives.
Every choice a tragedy of excluded possibility, we
were thwarted by ourselves. Let these never
poems cast you skyward, darling. Be a star,
as small gods are with their cold gaze,
their tendency to self-regard.

CIRCUS MAXIMUS

The fat men jog the circuit once,
Ricotta Tremulous. A long-fallen empire
teaches the folly of fighting against
what will be. Tourists come
to learn how the Romans wiped
themselves (with pinecones).

How they shat and ate: the shared
gifts of our two late civilizations.

In these matted grasses, Ovid writes,
the Sabine women were raped.
(*Rapere* meant to seize or drag away.)
In exchange for losing everything,
the mothers earned the right
to bear free sons and maybe mother
soldiers, if the gods were good.

SABAUDIA

The delicate Italian town
preserves its symbols—
bushels of wheat and axes
stamped on manhole covers.
The Fascists have fled their utopia,
the block's leased to Gypsies and Africans
whose cash crop is kiwis.
Without meaning to, I files
these facts for you,
ambassador to a country
that no longer exists.

ASMA

*For Asma Safi (1985–2013), who worked as a translator in
Afghanistan, suffered from a congenital heart condition, and died in a
taxi on her way to the hospital in Kabul. Before she died, she asked her
father to bury her body in the family village in Kunar Province, which
was held by the Taliban. Her father feared that her funeral might draw
the unwanted attention of an American drone operator who could
mistake Asma's burial for a Taliban meeting. Despite his fears, and
although the Taliban did attend to pay respects, there was no incident.*

Again we think of your father,
shouldering your shrouded body
in a taxi toward the war—

You'd asked to be buried
in your grandfather's village,
ground so rife with disaster

that two or three gathered
could draw the reaper's eye.
Your father knew a daughter

can be martyred, sure as any son.
Your life was forfeit
to a country come undone.

SNOW IN ROME

on the synagogue's dome, the palms, the pines,
the travertine spine of Aurelian Wall
against which our transgressions pile:
We gossiped, we snubbed a dinner guest.
So much for self-awareness;
all walls speak of weakness,
the need to mount defense.
This one's marred by cannonballs,
scarified by trilobites embedded
in its stone. Their shells are gone.
What's left is what's missing. A fossil is
a negative. We hate being human,
depleted by absence. Once
I had the sense to hold herself apart.

NO MOTHER IS GOOD ENOUGH

Maybe the baby was not the idea,
and Piero's pregnant Madonna
taped to the closet's rear wall
isn't about Jesus or having a child,
but what will burst forth from the unlaced dress,
less dress than mind, as Hanuman,
the monkey god, held the world
in his mouth, singing, *In the fullness*
of time, my darlings, my humankind,
all things will be and not be.

RENUNCIATION

There are days while she rakes the manger's hay
that the crowd of lepers and weirdos
waiting for a glimpse of salvation
wends down the muddy path
in a parade of wretchedness
farther than her human eye can see.

She curses the vain angel
who wanted to be off to glory
and away from the room encoded
with the odor of women.

Stroking his cheek with the lily,
distracted by his beauty,
the angel didn't hear her quiet *no*.

SHIELDMAIDEN

In 2013, in the Italian town of Tarquinia, archaeologists
uncovered a 2,600-year-old Etruscan tomb. Inside were the
bodies of a man, believed, at first, to be a warrior prince, and that
of a woman misunderstood to be his consort. After closer inspection,
the archaeologists established that the woman was the warrior.

The entombed soldier proved not a prince,
but a woman holding the lance. A real killer.
Her grave calls others into question
along with our readings of figures on Etruscan vases.
In the Greek depiction, the darker a woman's skin
the higher her status.

                              Consider Sheba,
the Ethiopian queen who came to Solomon with riddles—
hillot in Aramaic also means hard questions.

Perhaps she asked the king about the future of her
possessions:
                         who, in their shared tomb, would hold
the golden lance, and who raise their eventual baby?
                          And he replied,
                              Let's split it.

4

TREE,

might you offer us wisdom,
standing with outstretched limbs
as a red-headed woodpecker lights
on your trunk and needles its beak
into the joins of your bark?

You could dispatch its feathery bones
with the toss of a bough
and no one would know
that it wasn't the wind.

Under your lower branches,
we sit; a physical practice
to quiet our mind: un-muscling,
the opposite of every behavior
we've been rewarded for.

GEOGRAPHIC II

America,
we turn to you uneasy and unreconciled,
unwilling to practice the sad, rotten
soft-shoe of longing
for elsewhere. Teach us
to align our will with what is.

INNER ÉMIGRÉ

Accustomed to hostile interiors,
we clock the leer
of the tyrant's false welcome
framed on the wall in Arrivals.

The national anthem:
the crackle and tick of a line
being listened to. Our minds,
it turns out, are also terrible country.

We turn to the wisdom of elsewhere.
In the bookstore, we find
Post-Apocalyptic Fiction
shelved in Current Events.

ARION AND THE DOLPHIN

In a time of tyranny, on Lesbos in the seventh century BC,
 the singer Arion,
known for his wild, Dionysian runes, sailed to Sicily
 with a band of Corinthian
brigands. Hearing them plot to rob and toss him
 overboard, he offered them
gold in exchange for his breath. Unmoved, they
 countered with a choice:
either drown or die on board, so they might bury his
 body to honor the gods.
Arion moved to the stern, and facing crisis, forsook
 Dionysus and lifted his song
to Apollo, then he leapt into the waves. Moved by the
 singer's measured order,
Apollo's dolphin rose from the salt to carry Arion back
 to Corinth and the tyrant's court,
where the singer told his tale. Fake news, the tyrant
 Periander said,
until the brigands returned, and their amazement at
 seeing Arion alive betrayed
their crime. There was for a time, according to
 Herodotus, a dolphin in bronze,

a rider on its back, at a place called Taenarum. The myth,
    of course, outlived
the statue of the myth; there's nothing left, not even the
    stub of a fin.

LOVE POEM FOR A MATURE AUDIENCE

Tugs push barges up and down the Hudson.
A train's gaunt whistle haunts the shore.
The working world's not working
anymore. Broke so long
it isn't the obsolete bridges
that keep us apart; it's our lack
of infrastructure. We're born
soft-boned, our endocrines
disrupted. We stand
for nothing; our spans
of attention spliced to a blip.
Across the water, the cars
of New Jersey shuttle
toward a day that
doesn't matter; boats
drift from their slips.

SLOUGH

In The Pilgrim's Progress, *John Bunyan describes the Slough of Despond as* "this miry Slough is such a place as cannot be mended." *This is the place where Christian grows trapped in remorse regarding his sins. Many others have referred to Bunyan's slough— among them, Louisa May Alcott, C. S. Forester, W. Somerset Maugham, and, more recently, the video wizards Jeff Kaplan, Rob Pardo, and Tom Chilton, creators of the game* World of Warcraft.

We pilgrims know one another by the lines
around our mouths set by the hard march
through the slough. A hard March,
and April proves no easier . . . and then
today, a boat at the slough's edge.
Funny, we think, wading into the sedge,
the tender was never tucked in these rushes
before, or perhaps, distracted by
disappointment in ourselves, we missed it,
its weathered gunwales, the amber water.

Let us be Moses, we laugh.
The day is suddenly conscious, or we
suddenly conscious that the day
has always been so. Electric with joy,
we climb in, push out of the mire,
only to find we're oarless. No matter.

Consider Moses and Oedipus,
and other famous babies
who floated downriver
toward princesses
and whores.

Also Osiris,
after being murdered by his brother,
floated north along the Nile,
to Byblos, where the god's body grew
into the base of a tamarisk.
A king cut the tree down
to carve his palace lintel.
We could do worse.

ODE TO THUCYDIDES

To love our husband is to welcome
his departures, to cherish
the back of him, his shoulders,
and beneath, a form accustomed
to rising early in pursuit of facts
that, strung together, assemble a truth.

Those tied to his body
must also relinquish our grasp.

This task is easier for us than for others.
We know the solace the eye finds
in places unindicted by familiarity:
scraps of meat pinned among laundry,
men with birds in their mouths
linger in a being. A being
is nothing other than what lingers.

KEY WEST

In a brackish inlet along Route 1,
a pod of bored dolphins paints T-shirts
and pretends to be balloons
with the air running out,
thrashing about and farting
from their mouths. It's true
they seem to be smiling;
it's also the shape of their jaw.
Up close, they do like applause.
It could be that lunch comes after.
There's no looking at a dolphin and not knowing
this creature is smarter than we are.
Their mothers name them,
a watery staccato of clicks and squeaks.

They are also conscious breathers,
they think to take in air—unlike
the rest of us, for whom consciousness
of anything is rare, let alone oxygen.
Yesterday, we watched a wild pair
play with our boat. Their shadows
darkened just before they broke
the surface. They stayed close
though no one was feeding them.
They could have swum away.

LITTLE GIDDING

We think of you there and earlier,
misplaced, praying away a fervent youth,
whickering into the darkness in a hard-won tongue
as if the Aramaic might arouse God.
We were born with an abiding loneliness—
a tendency to wake from dreams, the soul's sap stirred,
returned mid-conversation to this secondary world

where we, less certain of ourselves,
our relevance, spend days misunderstanding
what we're yearning for—which isn't to be praised,
but to praise. Love's the flame unsought,
half-sought, half-bidden then unbidden,
half-hidden and revealed against our will,
against the grinding mind that tells us otherwise—

a train chuffing out of the station *not enough not*
enough not enough—you've learned where
the exits are, descending laughing.
How do we surrender to this doubleness
with the humor also known as grace?

WHAT IF THE APOCALYPSE WERE SUDDEN

We have watched the end begin
in distant lands, and when
it comes it comes as threads
of smoke rising on the horizon,
for days, years even. Uncertain
approach becomes a point
of neighborly discussion, like threat
of drought, or any bout
of bad weather. Other villages
burn. Mothers return to laundry,
leaving their suburban survivalism
half attended to—drawing down
from bottled waters, pilfering
the end times store of RXBARs,
reluctant to leave the requisite cash
in a drawer. It seems too much till
one day it's no metaphor. We wake
to the snap of a black flag over the door.

METAMORPHOSIS

The mimosa trees misunderstand
the New Year's heat and burst
into mustard tufts across the garden.

Poor trees, like nine-year-old girls
who've grown breasts. It's death
pressing under tender flesh.
In I's day most of us feared tumors
and we were in season.

Long ago, a girl could become a tree.
Root hairs branched from her toes,
her torqued curls gnarled into limbs.
She thickened, as we do,
in this age of self-defense.

HIGH ABOVE ALL NATIONS

A body swings from the palace window,
limp neck and arms flung back in parody
of ecstasy mark a dynasty's end.

To what purpose who can tell, and the man
who knows what his unseen eyes had fixed on
in the raucous firmament; which star

in the madness of stars had beckoned saying—
no, not saying, no need to say—*Come.*

ELEPHANT

Who was I
but the blind one
groping the elephant's leg
and arguing with phantoms
as to the shape of his trunk.
Lesser minds might favor happiness.

TOWARD A NEW YEAR

We set alight two paper boats
and nudged them up the wave's face
to be carried, dream-laden, toward the kingdom
of drowned gods.

        Of gods, we bore few illusions,
having borne loss upon loss, having torn scales

from our skin; some days fish, others dragon—
fresh flesh stings raw beneath both.

        We'd learned to be gentle with yearning.
We were with the hulls: holding one another's dreams
and sending a finger length of flame into the rough bay.
Need I say against all odds—

        a pinch of fire, an ocean.